Ellis Island

The Story of a Gateway to America

Patriotic Symbols of America

Ellis Island
The Story of a Gateway to America

Hal Marcovitz

Mason Crest
Philadelphia

Mason Crest
450 Parkway Drive, Suite D
Broomall, PA 19008
www.masoncrest.com

Printed and bound in the United States of America.

CPSIA Compliance Information: Batch #PSA2014. For further information, contact Mason Crest at 1-866-MCP-Book.

Publisher's note: all quotations in this book come from original sources, and contain the spelling and grammatical inconsistencies of the original text.

First printing
1 3 5 7 9 8 6 4 2

Library of Congress Cataloging-in-Publication Data

on file at the Library of Congress

ISBN: 978-1-4222-3123-4 (hc)
ISBN: 978-1-4222-8746-0 (ebook)

Patriotic Symbols of America series ISBN: 978-1-4222-3117-3

Contents

KEY ICONS TO LOOK FOR:

Text-dependent questions: These questions send the reader back to the text for more careful attention to the evidence presented there.

Words to understand: These words with their easy-to-understand definitions will increase the reader's understanding of the text, while building vocabulary skills.

Series glossary of key terms: This back-of-the book glossary contains terminology used throughout this series. Words found here increase the reader's ability to read and comprehend higher-level books and articles in this field.

Research projects: Readers are pointed toward areas of further inquiry connected to each chapter. Suggestions are provided for projects that encourage deeper research and analysis.

Sidebars: This boxed material within the main text allows readers to build knowledge, gain insights, explore possibilities, and broaden their perspectives by weaving together additional information to provide realistic and holistic perspectives.

Patriotic Symbols and American History

Symbols are not merely ornaments to admire—they also tell us stories. If you look at one of them closely, you may want to find out why it was made and what it truly means. If you ask people who live in the society in which the symbol exists, you will learn some things. But by studying the people who created that symbol and the reasons why they made it, you will understand the deepest meanings of that symbol.

The United States owes its identity to great events in history, and the most remarkable of our patriotic symbols are rooted in these events. The struggle for independence from Great Britain gave America the Declaration of Independence, the Liberty Bell, the American flag, and other images of freedom. The War of 1812 gave the young country a song dedicated to the flag, "The Star-Spangled Banner," which became our national anthem. Nature gave the country its national animal, the bald eagle. These symbols established the identity of the new nation, and set it apart from the nations of the Old World.

To be emotionally moving, a symbol must strike people with a sense of power and unity. But it often takes a long time for a new symbol to be accepted by all the people, especially if there are older symbols that have gradually lost popularity. For example, the image of Uncle Sam has replaced Brother Jonathan, an earlier representation of the national will, while the Statue of Liberty has replaced Columbia, a woman who represented liberty to Americans in the early 19th century. Since then, Uncle Sam and the Statue of Liberty have endured and have become cherished icons of America.

Of all the symbols, the Statue of Liberty has perhaps the most curious story, for unlike other symbols, Americans did not create her. She was created by the French, who then gave her to America. Hence, she represented not what Americans thought of their country but rather what the French thought of America. It was many years before Americans decided to accept this French goddess of Liberty as a symbol for the United States and its special role among the nations: to spread freedom and enlighten the world.

This series of books is valuable because it presents the story of each of America's great symbols in a freshly written way and will contribute to the students' knowledge and awareness of them. It it to be hoped that this information will awaken an abiding interest in American history, as well as in the meanings of American symbols.

— Barry Moreno,
librarian and historian
Ellis Island/Statue of Liberty National Monument

 Words to Understand

famine—extreme scarcity of food leading to widespread hunger.

immigrant—a person who travels to another country for permanent residence.

quay—a landing place for a ship.

steerage—a place on a ship below deck where passengers paying low fares were housed, often near the ship's steering mechanism.

Immigrant families, with their belongings, wait to be processed at the Ellis Island Immigration Center. Millions of people seeking a new life in America passed through the doors of Ellis Island between 1892 and 1954.

The First Arrivals

In late December 1891, Annie Moore and her two brothers made their way down Deepwater *Quay* in their hometown of Queenstown in County Cork, Ireland. At the end of the quay, the S.S. *Nevada* sat gently in the water, waiting for the passengers to board.

Soon, the *Nevada* would shove off and steam west over the choppy waves of the Atlantic Ocean. Its final destination: New York City.

Annie was 14 years old. For the past three years, Annie and her brothers Anthony, 11, and Phillip, 7, had lived with relatives in County Cork. Their parents, Matthew and Mary Moore, had been living in New York, where they worked hard to save enough money to pay for the *steerage* passage to America for their children. Finally, the money arrived.

The Moore family wanted to leave Ireland because times were hard on the island. During the 19th century, *famine* had swept through Ireland. From 1845 to 1849, the country's important potato crop had failed. Suddenly, people didn't have enough to eat. More than a million Irish citizens died from starvation and disease. During the famine years, as many as 1.5 million Irish citizens left their country, many of them making their way to the United States.

Make Connections

Queenstown, the Irish town where Annie Moore departed for Ellis Island, was also the last port of call for the *Titanic* on the luxury liner's ill-fated maiden voyage across the Atlantic Ocean in 1912. Today, the city is known by its Gaelic name, Cobh.

Even after the famine ended, people continued to leave Ireland seeking a better life. Ireland was ruled by Great Britain, and there were few opportunities for Irish Catholics in their homeland. Many people had to leave Ireland in order to find work and raise their families in a place where they would not be persecuted by the government.

The S.S. *Nevada* had made the trip from Ireland to the United States many times. The ship had started ferrying *immigrants* across the Atlantic in 1869 and would continue making the trip until 1894.

Annie and her brothers arrived in New York Harbor on January 1, 1892—Annie's 15th birthday. Their ship sailed slowly past the Statue of Liberty, the 151-foot-tall gift from France that had been erected on Bedloe's Island just five years before to welcome immigrants to America. A year after Annie passed the statue, a poem written by Emma Lazarus was engraved into its pedestal. Titled "The New Colossus," the poem was intended to comfort the hearts of the frightened immigrants as they arrived at America's shores after their long journeys across the sea. The poem said:

> Give me your tired, your poor,
>> Your huddled masses yearning to breathe free,
> The wretched refuse of your teeming shore,
>> Send these, the homeless tempest-tost to me,
> I lift my lamp beside the golden door!

The *Nevada* dropped its anchor just a half-mile from the Statue of Liberty. Behind the *Nevada*, two other ships—the S.S. *City of Paris* and S.S. *Victoria*—also

---

KEY EVENT: Anne Moore Arrives in the U.S.

Annie Moore and her brothers Anthony and Phillip were the first immigrants processed at Ellis Island in 1892.

Following the medical examinations and interviews with immigration officers, the Moore children were soon reunited with their parents. They made their home at 32 Monroe Street in New York; later, the family moved to Indiana.

When she was 21, Annie met and married Patrick O'Connell. Annie and her husband moved to Texas, where they started a family and raised five children.

Sadly, she died in a train accident at the age of 46.

Today, there are two statues of Annie Moore and her brothers. One statue stands on Deepwater Quay in County Cork, Ireland. The other statue of Annie was erected on Ellis Island. It was molded in bronze by the artist Jeanne Rynhart. It depicts the fresh-faced girl from Ireland, one hand on her hat to hold it in place while she lifts her head to see the sights of New York Harbor, the other hand grasping the small suitcase that held the few possessions an immigrant could take aboard ship as she prepared to begin a new life in a far-off land.

prepared to drop anchors, each carrying hundreds of immigrants. Soon, the *John E. Moore*, a small transfer boat, came alongside the *Nevada* and 148 passengers from the steamship went aboard for a short cruise to a dock on the southern tip of Ellis Island, where the United States government was opening a new immigration center. The passengers who had crossed the Atlantic Ocean on the *Nevada* would be the first immigrants to be processed at Ellis Island.

The *John E. Moore* arrived at the dock. The gangplank was lowered. Annie found herself right at the rail of the *John E. Moore*. A sailor lifted it, and Annie hurried down the gangplank; she was first off the boat, trailed closely behind by her brothers.

Bells rang and whistles sounded. A band played patriotic music. Annie was met at the foot of the gangplank by Colonel John B. Weber, the new commissioner for immigration for Ellis Island. Weber presented Annie with a gold piece worth $10—a considerable sum in those days. Annie told Colonel Weber that she would "never part with it, but will always keep it as a pleasant memento of the occasion."

Twelve million immigrants passed through Ellis Island on their way to new lives in America. Today, more than 110 million Americans—roughly one-third of the total U.S. population—are descended from the immigrants who arrived at Ellis Island between 1892 and 1954, when the immigration center on the island closed.

And it all started with Annie Moore.

Text-Dependent Question

What was the name of the ship that carried Annie Moore and her brothers to the United States?

Research Project

Immigrants come to the United States for many specific reasons, but in general most immigrants are looking for greater freedom and work opportunities than are available in their home countries. Ask your parents and/or grandparents about the circumstances that brought your ancestors to America. Write a report explaining when, how, and why they came, what they did when they first arrived, and how they eventually assimilated into American culture.

 Words to Understand

alien—a foreign-born inhabitant of a country.

colonist—a member of a new settlement in a foreign land.

Congress—the lawmaking branch of United States government.

detainee—a person who is kept in custody.

Manhattan—one of five boroughs that make up New York City; the others are Staten Island, Queens, Brooklyn, and the Bronx.

Visitors walk through Great Hall, where the immigrants were processed at Ellis Island. The immigration station served as a port of entry to the United States from 1892 to 1954. Ellis Island's busiest year came in 1907, when 1.25 million immigrants were processed through Great Hall.

The Melting Pot

Immigrants had been making their way to America long before Annie and her brothers stepped off the gangplank of the *John E. Moore.*

Although they weren't the first, perhaps the most well-known immigrants were the 105 *colonists* from England who established the settlement of Jamestown in Virginia in 1607. Millions more have followed, drawn to America and its promise of religious, political, and cultural freedoms.

For years, the United States had few laws governing immigration. The federal government preferred to leave the matter in the hands of the state governments.

In 1819, the United States *Congress* passed the first national law to control immigration. This law regulated rules and standards for steerage passengers on sailing ships. Starting in 1820, several states enacted their own immigration laws. However, the U.S. Supreme Court usually threw out those laws, ruling that the Constitution had given Congress authority over relations with foreign countries. Finally, in 1876, the Supreme Court asked Congress to adopt an overall immigration law for the United States.

Congress finally acted in 1882, providing for federal supervision of immigration. The new law charged a "head tax" of 50 cents on every *alien* who entered the country. Congress assigned the Treasury Department the job of administering the immigration program. The Treasury Department in turn contracted with the states

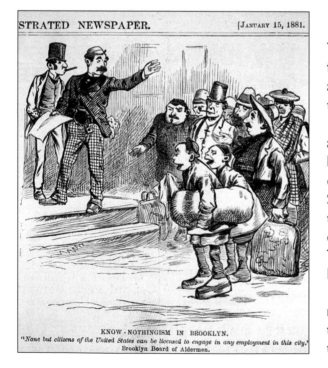

KNOW-NOTHINGISM IN BROOKLYN.
"*None but citizens of the United States can be licensed to engage in any employment in this city.*"
Brooklyn Board of Aldermen.

This political cartoon from 1881 shows an anti-immigrant attitude that emerged during the 19th century. It depicts a group of immigrants being told, "None but citizens of the United States can be licensed to engage in any employment in this city." The term "Know-Nothingism" refers to a 19th-century political movement that sought to restrict immigration to the United States.

to carry out the duties of accepting immigrants.

Congress was never satisfied with that arrangement. Each state had its own rules and policies. So in 1891, federal lawmakers established the Bureau of Immigration. They gave this new agency the power to oversee the arrival of immigrants.

For years, most immigrants had been making their way into the United States through New York Harbor simply because it was America's busiest port. These were the days before air travel; most people taking long trips from one continent to another did so aboard large ships capable of carrying hundreds of passengers.

In 1855, the state government in New York set up an immigration center at Castle Garden, a former military fort on the lower tip of *Manhattan* Island. When the federal government took control of immigration in 1882, Castle Garden continued to be the city's immigration center, operating under federal authorities.

By 1890, so many immigrants were arriving that it was clear the facilities at Castle Garden were no longer adequate. There were other problems with Castle Garden, too. For years, immigration officials had watched helplessly as ill-prepared immigrants stepped out of the doors of Castle Garden onto the busy streets of Manhattan. Many of them fell victim to the unsavory characters loitering near the Castle Garden doors, ready with a promise of easy wealth and adventure in the New World. Those con artists intended only to find a way to rob the immigrants of what little money or valuables they owned.

So officials searched around the port area of New York for a better location. They were drawn to a tiny stretch of land in the harbor known as Ellis Island.

Ellis Island seemed like an ideal location, specifically because it was an island. By keeping the immigrants on an island for several hours, federal officials knew they could shelter them from the con artists in the city until the newcomers were better prepared to deal with them.

VITAL AGENCY: Immigration Agencies

Today, all immigration into the United States is regulated by the Department of Homeland Security (DHS), a government agency created after the September 11, 2001, terrorist attacks. DHS absorbed most of the functions of the old U.S. Immigration and Naturalization Service (INS), which had replaced the U.S. Bureau of Immigration in 1933.

Today, the Department of Homeland Security operates three agencies that oversee various matters related to immigration. U.S. Citizenship and Immigration Services (USCIS) is responsible for most of the paperwork related to legal immigration to the United States, such as admitting people from other countries to live permanently in the U.S. or granting naturalized American citizenship. USCIS processes immigrant visa petitions, naturalization petitions, and asylum and refugee applications. USCIS currently has more than 15,000 employees working in over 250 locations across the United States.

The other two DHS agencies are U.S. Immigration and Customs Enforcement (ICE) and U.S. Customs and Border Protection (CBP). They are responsible for enforcing laws related to immigration, and preventing undocumented immigrants from entering the United States.

The three-acre island had been known originally as "Kioshk" or Gull Island by the Mohican Indians. In 1628, Dutch settlers renamed it Oyster Island when they found rich deposits of oysters along its thin beaches. In 1765, a pirate named Anderson was hanged on the island, prompting the settlers to rename the island Gibbet Island (a gibbet was a device used in colonial times to execute prisoners). Finally, in 1785, a merchant named Samuel Ellis bought the island. He died in 1794; in his will, Ellis passed the island onto the unborn child of his pregnant daughter. The child was born but died in infancy. Ellis' descendants argued over ownership of the island for the next several years.

With the threat of the War of 1812 gathering over the United States, New York's state government believed New York City could be vulnerable to British attack. So in 1808 the state bought Ellis Island from the Ellis family for $10,000 and erected Fort Gibson, which operated there until 1861.

After the Civil War, the navy used the base to store arms, powder, and ammunition. However, neighbors whose homes in New Jersey were just a few hundred yards away complained to the government. They were afraid that the old fort could explode and damage their houses. The navy moved its munitions out. By the time immigration officials looked over the place, Fort Gibson was little more than an old rotting hulk of a building.

Immigration officials decided to tear down Fort

Gibson and erect a new immigration station on the island. Congress allowed $75,000 for the project. A large, three-story reception building constructed of Georgia pine and a slate roof was the largest building erected on the island. Another building contained a small house where *detainees* could stay. These were people who would be held on the island if authorities suspected they had medical or legal problems. Immigration officials wanted to prevent people with contagious diseases from entering the country. Also, they wanted to make sure immigrants were not outlaws who were running from the law in their own countries. Such people would be detained until their medical and legal questions could be cleared up.

Immigrants who have been deemed undesirable wait in the detention pen at Ellis Island to be returned to their home countries, circa 1902.

Other buildings erected on the island included a small hospital, a cafeteria, a baggage station, and a power plant. The dock was built on the southern tip of the island. Landing boats and barges carried the immigrants from their ships to the dock. Also arriving and departing from the dock were ferries that would take the immigrants from the island to New York city. In the city, they could meet relatives at dockside or board trains for other areas of the country.

About 500 people had jobs on the island. There were immigration officers who interviewed the immigrants, clerks, guards, gatekeepers, watchmen, maintenance workers, cooks, and janitors. There were also jobs for dozens of interpreters, because people arriving at Ellis Island spoke many languages, and few of them understood English.

In 1892, architects inspecting the new immigration center on Ellis Island complained the building was so poorly constructed it would likely fall down within five years. Their prediction proved accurate: the building burned down in 1897.

The island opened January 1, 1892, when the passengers from the *Nevada, City of Paris,* and *Victoria* stepped onto the island.

On June 15, 1897, Ellis Island was temporarily closed when a fire broke out in the kitchen and quickly swept through the island's wooden buildings. The immigration center and other buildings were leveled. Luckily, there were no injuries.

Congress responded by providing $600,000 to erect new brick-and-iron buildings. It took three years to rebuild the center. The new Ellis Island reopened in December 1900. In the meantime, immigrants had been directed through the old Castle Garden facility.

The main building, Great Hall, was 338 feet long, 168 feet wide and featured four cupola-type towers. The main Registry Room measured 200 feet by 100 feet and was 56 feet high. It was in this hall that immigrants lined up to be interviewed by immigration officers. The building also housed a dormitory, offices, record rooms, a railroad ticket office, and a huge baggage center. Other buildings, including a medical center, bathhouse, and cafeteria, were added over the years. By the time the island closed in 1954, it contained 35 separate buildings.

As Ellis Island prepared to reopen after the 1897 fire, the federal government wanted to clean up more than just the rubble from the blaze. Theodore Roosevelt had been unhappy with reports of corruption at the island. Roosevelt was a former governor of New York who had become president of the United States in 1901. He heard that some immigrants had been forced to pay bribes to immigration officers for permission to enter the United States. Railroad agents on the island

Make Connections

In 1907, the S.S. *Baltic* carried 1,000 single women searching for husbands to Ellis Island. Many of the women chose husbands right in Great Hall, where they exchanged wedding vows.

charged high fees for tickets because newcomers had no idea the real cost of the tickets. They paid the inflated prices, with the agents pocketing the difference. There was a money exchange office on the island, where immigrants could trade the money they brought with them from home for American dollars. Employees in the money exchange office simply lied about the rates of exchange, keeping the difference.

Roosevelt appointed William Williams, a young New York lawyer, as the new commissioner of immigration for Ellis Island. Williams booted out the corrupt workers and insisted that employees on Ellis Island treat the immigrants with "kindness and consideration."

Soon, the government realized Ellis Island was too small. To enlarge the island, thousands of tons of dirt were dumped into the harbor. The dirt was from the digging of New York City's subway system. Eventually, the immigration center at Ellis Island covered 27 acres and included two smaller islands. One of those islands housed a hospital erected in 1913 to detain patients with contagious diseases.

Text-Dependent Question
Why was the immigration center at Castle Garden closed?

Research Project
Today, anyone born in a foreign country who wants to become a U.S. Citizen immigrants must first take a naturalization test that shows they have learned about American history and government. A practice exam is available at http://www.uscis.gov/us-citizenship/naturalization-test. Can you pass the test to become a citizen?

Words to Understand

deportation—the expulsion of an alien from a country.

favus—a disease of the scalp, often causing the skin to dry and become scabbed.

haven—a place of safety or comfort.

lice—small insects known to make their homes in human skin, sucking the blood of hosts and spreading disease.

tuberculosis—a disease of the lungs; if left untreated, will cause lungs and other organs to deteriorate.

trachoma—a contagious infection of the eyelids and surrounding area; if left untreated, the disease could result in blindness.

stowaway—one who hides aboard a ship or airplane to obtain free passage.

An inspector examines the eyes of a new arrival to Ellis Island in the early 1900s. For many immigrants, Ellis Island was a place of hope; it was also a place of fear, for those with diseases or health problems might be refused entry into the United States.

Island of Hope

For millions of immigrants, Ellis Island was the "Island of Hope," the gate at the end of a long and tiring voyage to religious or political freedom. For some immigrants, though, it was the "Island of Tears." There were many reasons immigrants were turned away from America, forced to return to their native countries.

For most of the immigrants, their experience on Ellis Island was over within a few hours. They made their way quickly through the medical examinations and interviews with immigration officers and were able to move on. But some people were detained. They might have to wait for a night, or for several days or weeks.

When the immigrants stepped off the barges at the south dock, their first steps on Ellis Island were taken up

Immigrants carry their luggage up the ramp from their barge toward the Ellis Island Immigration Station.

a long wooden ramp that led to Great Hall. Once in the building, they were directed up a flight of stairs where men were separated from women and children.

The climb up the stairs was known as the "Six-Second Physical." Doctors and nurses watched from the top of the stairs, weeding out people who seemed out of breath. These immigrants were suspected of carrying the disease *tuberculosis*, and they were taken to a hospital. Physicians were also on the lookout for scarlet fever, smallpox, yellow fever, and measles.

After climbing the stairs, the immigrants found themselves in the cavernous Registry Room, where they waited in long lines separated by iron-pipe railings. Later, the alleys created by the railings were replaced by long wooden benches. "It looked just like a church with pews," remembered Joseph Haas, who arrived from Germany as a 14-year-old in 1922. "You just slid down on the pews until you got to the end."

Eventually, the immigrants would hear the words "Next! Next! Next!" shouted in a dozen languages as their turns came up to leave the benches and meet with immigration officers.

"Every so often, somebody called out names of immigrants to be questioned," said William Chase, who arrived from Russia in 1914. "I was nervous because it was so noisy. I couldn't hear the names and was afraid I would miss mine and remain there forever."

An immigration officer first performed a quick medical check, looking for *trachoma*. The test for this eye disease involved raising the immigrant's eyelids with fingers or sometimes hairpins or buttonhooks—it was often quite painful. Next, scalps were inspected for *favus*, a fungal infection.

Immigration officers made chalk marks on the clothes of immigrants who were suspected of having health problems. An "E"

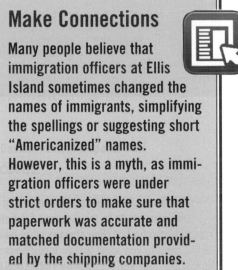

Make Connections

Many people believe that immigration officers at Ellis Island sometimes changed the names of immigrants, simplifying the spellings or suggesting short "Americanized" names. However, this is a myth, as immigration officers were under strict orders to make sure that paperwork was accurate and matched documentation provided by the shipping companies.

made with chalk meant eye problems, an "H" meant heart problems, "X" meant mental retardation and an "X" in a circle meant insanity. A woman marked "Pg" meant she was pregnant. To prove their mental competency, immigrants were asked to put together a puzzle of a wooden ship.

"I was jostled and dragged and shoved and shouted at," recalled immigrant M.E. Ravage. It was hectic, to be sure, and the medical examinations were often probing.

VITAL FIGURE: The Lady in the Harbor

The Statue of Liberty was a gift from the people of France to the United States to celebrate America's democratic way of life. The 151-foot statue was sculpted by Frédéric Auguste Bartholdi using sheets of copper over an iron framework designed by Gustave Eiffel, who would go on to design the famous Eiffel Tower in Paris.

The statue was erected in 1886 on Bedloe's Island in New York Harbor, about a half-mile from Ellis Island. All 12 million immigrants who passed through Ellis Island on their way into the United States sailed under the torch of "Lady Liberty."

Other features of the statue include a crown of seven rays to represent the seven continents and seven seas; a tablet of laws inscribed with the Roman numerals for "1776," and broken shackles at her feet to symbolize the broken bonds of oppression.

In 1893, the Statue of Liberty became an important symbol for immigration when the words of Emma Lazarus's poem "The New Colossus" were inscribed in the pedestal.

The immigrants were also required to strip so officers could check their bodies and clothing for *lice*. "Every morning they came around to delouse us," said Fannie Kligerman, a young Jewish girl who arrived from Russia in 1905. "You know what that means? Our things were taken off, we were naked and deloused. . . . They took all our clothes, nice dresses. As soon as we entered America, we had to put them in the garbage."

Many volunteers helped the immigration officers look after the interests of the new arrivals. The American Red Cross, Young Women's Christian Association, Salvation Army, and dozens of other welfare and religious groups sent volunteers to the island, bringing along coffee and doughnuts as well as used clothes. The volunteers helped track down lost luggage, wandering children, and relatives waiting on the mainland. Lillian Kaiz, who arrived at the age of seven in 1922 from Russia, recalled: "The first night they were celebrating Christmas. They had a movie. I had never seen one. And there was Santa Claus. And we got tiny little gifts. All the beauty of Christmas suddenly hit me."

If the immigrants were found to be healthy, they next had to answer questions intended to identify people with legal or social problems. While the United States may have been a *haven* for people seeking religious or cultural freedom, violent criminals were not welcome.

The immigration officers were also looking for immigrant workers who had been rounded up by

Today, the descendants of immigrants who were processed at Ellis Island can have their parents' names added to the American Immigrant Wall of Honor at the park.

unscrupulous factory bosses who paid their passage over to obtain cheap labor. If these immigrants were allowed to pass through Ellis Island on their way to the factories, they would not be paid for their work, and would instead be expected to work off their steerage fares in the factories. Those immigrants were sent back.

Immigration officers kept an eye out for *stowaways* who hid aboard ships. They also turned up many immigrants who had no money, no relatives in the United States, no job prospects, and no place to live. Because the government feared these immigrants would become "public charges," they were sent back to their home countries.

Still, eight out of 10 immigrants made it through the interviews and were able to leave Ellis Island within hours of their arrival. At the southern tip of the island, they boarded ferries for the trip across the harbor to Manhattan, where they met friends and relatives or caught trains in the city. Others took the ferry to the railroad station in Hoboken, New Jersey, where they bought tickets to trains headed for other American cities.

Back on the island, the detainees found themselves living in dormitory rooms equipped with beds outfitted with wire-mesh or canvas mattresses. Each dormitory held up to 50 beds.

"I cried all night," recalled Maljan Chavoor, a 12-year-old Turkish boy who was detained in a dormitory for one night in 1922. "I grew up in a hurry. The next day, I told my mother what happened. She said, 'Son, everything is all right. Now we are in America.'"

Most of the immigrants who were detained were eventually able to move on as well. Just 2 percent of the immigrants who arrived at Ellis Island were *deported*, or forced to return to their native countries.

Text-Dependent Question
What were some of the reasons that immigrants were detained at Ellis Island?

Research Project
Imagine that you had to travel to another country, and could only take one suitcase with you. What would you take, and why? Create a list of your possessions, and explain the reason for bringing each item, and how it would help you to live in an unfamiliar place.

 Words to Understand

emigrate—to leave one country and settle in another.

ethnic group—group of people of the same race or nationality who share a common culture.

quota—In immigration, a limit set by law on the number of people from a specific country permitted to enter the United States.

During the 1920s, immigration to the United States slowed because of "quota laws," that determined how many people could enter the United States each year. The total number of immigrants allowed was a percentage based on the number of people of each **ethnic group** already living in America. For example, for every 100,000 Italian-Americans, 3,000 people from Italy (3 percent) would be allowed to enter the country each year.

The Golden Door

In December 17, 1900, Ellis Island reopened after the disastrous fire that swept had through the facility some three years before. On that day, 2,251 immigrants walked up the ramp at the south dock and were processed through Great Hall.

Over the next 50 years, immigrants would arrive elsewhere in America. Boston, Massachusetts, and Savannah, Georgia, were two important ports of call for the steamships ferrying passengers from the European nations. On the West Coast, most immigrants from China, Japan, and other Asian nations entered the country through San Francisco, California.

But there was no question that Ellis Island served as the "Golden Door" for many immigrants seeking new homes in America.

Most came from Europe. In 1890, two years before Ellis Island was in operation, there were 9.2 million people living in America who had been born in a foreign country. Ten years later that number had jumped to 10.3 million people—meaning that more than a million more people had arrived during the last decade of the 19th century. Nearly 900,000 of those people had come from European countries.

It was easy to see why. There were few democracies in Europe at that time. Most European countries were ruled by kings whose families had held their thrones for centuries. They were now losing their grip on power and were finding it increasingly hard to provide for their people. Often, they turned to violence to keep order. In the Russian Empire, the government sometimes encouraged pogroms, or organized attacks on Jewish citizens during the late 19th and early 20th centuries. The outbreak of World War I in Europe in 1914 led to poverty

Physicians at Ellis Island examine a group of Jewish immigrants, circa 1907. (the eye chart on the wall has Hebrew characters.) Many Jews emigrated from Russia and Eastern Europe to escape persecution in their home countries.

and suffering for millions of people on both sides of the conflict. By 1920, 1.6 million Germans had *emigrated* to America. Italy also suffered from corruption and harsh rulers, and by 1930, nearly 1.9 million people living in America had been born in Italy.

Make Connections

During World War I, about 1,800 Germans were held in custody on Ellis Island.

There were problems elsewhere in the world that prompted immigration. The poverty in Ireland that Annie Moore and her brothers fled in 1892 prompted others to leave as well. By 1900, some 1.6 million people living in the United States had been born in Ireland.

Most people who arrived through Ellis Island stayed in or around New York City. Although immigration officials at Ellis Island provided transportation for immigrants to train stations in Manhattan and New Jersey, it is clear that most of the arriving aliens decided their long voyage across the Atlantic was all the traveling they intended to do. In 1890, two years before Ellis Island's first year of operation, the number of people living in New York who had been born in a foreign country was 639,943. In 1910, the United States Census Bureau reported that 1,944,357 people living in New York were foreign-born.

That number continued to rise until 1940, when the foreign-born population of New York began to recede, in part due to restrictions on travel placed on European citizens as their nations prepared for World War II.

Overall immigration to the United States started to ebb in the 1920s. In those years, some politicians worried that native-born Americans were losing jobs to immigrants, so Congress passed several anti-immigration laws. In 1921, the so-called "*Quota* Laws" were passed, followed by the "Native Origins Act" of 1924. Restrictions from these two measures limited the number of new immigrants permitted to enter the United States. Later, these laws were repealed.

By World War II, due to the legal restrictions on immigration as well as the near lack of travel out of war zones, immigration through Ellis Island was virtually non-existent. During the war years, captured enemy sailors were housed on the island. The facility also served as a training center for the Coast Guard. After the war, Ellis Island reopened to immigration.

However, airliners soon replaced steamships as the preferred method of travel, and fewer immigrants had to enter America through a seaport. In 1954, a Norwegian merchant seaman named Arne Peterssen was the last immigrant to walk out of Ellis Island.

For years, the government did nothing with the old immigration station. The island fell victim to vandals, looters, and hobos. The majestic Great Hall, exposed to the elements in the middle of New York Harbor, had turned into a rickety hulk on the verge of collapse.

In the 1970s, a number of efforts were initiated to raise money for the island's restoration. These projects all fell short of being able to raise the massive amount of money it would take to preserve Great Hall and the buildings on the island. Finally, in 1982, the Statue of Liberty–Ellis Island Centennial Commission was formed to undertake the job of not only restoring Ellis Island, but financing the long-overdue maintenance on the century-old Statue of Liberty as well.

When architect John Belle oversaw the restoration of Ellis Island during the 1980s, his aim was for the Great Hall to look "right" to past immigrants who walked through its

> ## Make Connections
>
> During the renovation of Ellis Island in the 1980s, construction workers dug up bones of Indians buried on the island hundreds of years before; Native American leaders were called in to re-bury the bones.

doors again. "We researched every file, every archive we could for any reference to the building," he said. "All the materials, the colors, the textures, had to be right."

By 1990, the commission had raised $156 million to restore the island, and workers had transformed the old Great Hall into the Ellis Island Immigration Museum.

Text-Dependent Question
What were the Quota Laws?

Research Project
After World War I, American immigration policy favored people from Western Europe over those from Eastern Europe, Asia, Latin America, or Africa. Using the Internet, look for information on racial attitudes and immigration in the 1920s and 1930s. Write a report explaining why some Americans wanted to prevent certain racial or national groups from becoming U.S. citizens. Use data to support your conclusions.

On October 29, 2012, Ellis Island was flooded by a storm surge that accompanied Hurricane Sandy. The storm caused extensive damage to buildings and the exhibits inside. Some parts of Ellis Island were reopened to visitors in late 2013, but most of the collection remained stored elsewhere until 2014.

"God Bless America"

Millions of immigrants made their homes in America, started families, and prospered.

Elia Kazan arrived in 1913 from Greece. He was four years old when his family led him through Great Hall. Kazan went on to become one of America's greatest movie directors, winning two Academy Awards.

Born in Ireland, Edward Flanagan was 18 years old when he stepped onto Ellis Island's south dock. He studied for the priesthood in Maryland and then became the assistant pastor at a church in Omaha, Nebraska. In 1917, Father Flanagan established his "Home for Homeless Boys." Later, he moved the home about 10 miles outside Omaha and renamed it "Boys Town."

Felix Frankfurter was 12 years old when he arrived at

Felix Frankfurter, an Austrian immigrant, served on the U.S. Supreme Court from 1939 to 1962.

Ellis Island in 1894. An immigrant from Austria, Frankfurter studied at Harvard University and became a lawyer. In 1939, President Franklin D. Roosevelt selected Frankfurter as a justice of the U.S. Supreme Court.

Knute Rockne was born in Voss, Norway. He arrived at Ellis Island in 1893 at the age of five. While attending college at Notre Dame University in Indiana, Rockne won a place on the football team. In 1913, as a captain of the team, he revolutionized the game forever when he introduced the forward pass as an offensive weapon. Later, Rockne went on to become the legendary coach of the Notre Dame "Fighting Irish."

Israel Baline, a Russian Jew, arrived at Ellis Island in 1893 at the age of five. He was musically talented, and found himself earning a living as a singing waiter in New York restaurants. When he was 23 years old, he published the song "Alexander's Ragtime Band," which became a hit and established him as one of the nation's most popular songwriters. Everybody recognized him by his professional name, Irving Berlin.

Irving Berlin lived to be 101 years old. His body of work includes the music and lyrics for such Broadway shows and movies as *Annie Get Your Gun, Call Me Madam, Easter Parade, Top Hat,* and *White Christmas.*

But his most beloved songs are his *patriotic* tunes—each song celebrating the freedoms and opportunities of America. "A patriotic song is an emo-

Composer Irving Berlin, who was five when he came through Ellis Island, wrote many patriotic songs.

tion and you must not embarrass an audience with it, or they will hate your guts," Berlin once said.

From Irving Berlin's pen came such songs as "Arms for the Love of America," "This is the Army, Mr. Jones," and "I Left My Heart at the Stage Door Canteen." And, certainly, his best known song of all: "God Bless America."

Text-Dependent Questions
What college was Knute Rockne associated with? What did he become nationally known for?

Research Project
In 2008, the library at Ellis Island was named for a famous entertainer, Bob Hope, who had beeen processed at Ellis Island when his family came to America in 1908. In your local library, look for biographical information about Bob Hope, and write a report about his life. How did he become famous? What did he do that made the U.S. government want to honor him by naming the Ellis Island library in his honor?

Chronology

1785 Merchant Samuel Ellis buys a small island in New York Harbor known mostly for its rich oyster beds; renames it Ellis Island.

1808 New York State buys Ellis Island and erects Fort Gibson.

1891 Congress creates U.S. Bureau of Immigration to oversee the arrival of aliens; the federal government buys Ellis Island to establish a New York-area immigration center.

1892 Annie Moore becomes the first immigrant to pass through Ellis Island on January 1.

1897 The wooden buildings on Ellis Island burn down after a fire erupts in a kitchen on June 15.

1900 Ellis Island reopens on December 17 after new buildings are erected.

1907 1.25 million immigrants are processed at Ellis Island, the highest one-year total.

1921 Quota laws are passed limiting immigration; use of Ellis Island begins to decline.

1954 The immigration station on Ellis Island closes.

1982 Statue of Liberty-Ellis Island Commission is formed to restore the island and nearby statue.

1990 The Ellis Island Immigration Museum opens to public after a $156 million restoration of Ellis Island.

2001 After the September 11 terrorist attacks, Ellis Island and the Statue of Liberty are closed until new security measures can be put into place.

2008 The Ellis Island Museum library is named in memory of one of the most famous immigrants to pass through the station, Bob Hope, who came to America in 1908.

2012 In October, Hurricane Sandy causes major damage to the infrastructure of Ellis Island.

2014 Public access to exhibits at Ellis Island is restored.

Series Glossary

capstone—a stone used at the top of a wall or other structure.

cornerstone—the first stone placed at a spot where two walls meet, usually considered the starting point of construction.

dome—an element of architecture that resembles the hollow upper half of a sphere.

edifice—a large building with an imposing appearance.

facade—the decorative front of a building.

foundation—the stone and mortar base built below ground that supports a building, bridge, monument, or other structure.

hallowed—holy, consecrated, sacred, or revered.

keystone—the architectural piece at the crown of a vault or arch which marks its apex, locking the other pieces into position.

memorial—something designed to help people remember a person or event in history.

obelisk—a shaft of stone that tapers at the peak.

pantheon—a public building containing monuments to a nation's heroes.

pedestal—the base or support on which a statue, obelisk, or column is mounted.

portico—a roof supported by columns, usually extending out from a building.

rotunda—a large and high circular hall or room in a building, usually surmounted by a dome.

standard—a flag or banner that is adopted as an emblem or symbol by a nation.

symbol—an item that represents or stands for something else.

Further Reading

Cannato, Vincent J. *American Passage: The History of Ellis Island*. New York: HarperPerennial, 2010.

Cieslik, Thomas, et al, editors. *Immigration: A Documentary and Reference Guide*. Westport, Conn.: Greenhaven Press, 2008.

Conway, Lorie. *Forgotten Ellis Island: The Extraordinary Story of America's Immigrant Hospital*. New York: HarperCollins, 2007.

Hammerschmidt, Peter A. *History of American Immigration*. Philadelphia: Mason Crest, 2009.

Landau, Elaine. *Ellis Island*. New York: Children's Press, 2008.

Marcovitz, Hal. *The Statue of Liberty*. Philadelphia: Mason Crest, 2014.

Schell, Richard, et al. *U.S. Immigration Citizenship Q&A*. Naperville, Ill.: Sphinx Publishing, 2008.

Internet Resources

http://www.nps.gov/elis/index.htm

National Park Service website for Ellis Island, which is part of Statue of Liberty National Monument. The site historical information about Ellis Island, photos of the facility and those who passed through it, and information for those who wish to visit the park.

http://saveellisisland.org

Save Ellis Island is a nonprofit organization that is attempting to raise the $250 million needed to renovate and preserve 30 decaying buildings on the south side of the island, including the former hospital and the ferry terminal.

http://www.ellisisland.org

This website, provided by the Statue of Liberty-Ellis Island Foundation, enables people to search immigration records online to established in 1982 to raise money to renovate these American landmarks. Today the foundation remains dedicated to restoration, preservation, and education at Ellis Island and the Statue of Liberty.

http://www.usa.gov/visitors/about.shtml

This page provided by the U.S. government gives visitors an opportunity to learn about the United States of America, including links to information about patriotic symbols, American culture and history, government departments and agencies, and other interesting information.

Index

Index

Picture Credits

page
1:    used under license from
       Shutterstock, Inc.
3:    used under license from
       Shutterstock, Inc.
8:    Library of Congress
12:   Luis Santos/Shutterstock
14:   Songquan Deng/Shutterstock
16:   Library of Congress
20:   Library of Congress

24:   Library of Congress
26:   Library of Congress
28:   National Park Service
30:   Library of Congress
32:   Library of Congress
34:   Library of Congress
38:   U.S. National Park Service
40:   Library of Congress
41:   Library of Congress

Contributors

BARRY MORENO has been librarian and historian at the Ellis Island Immigration Museum and the Statue of Liberty National Monument since 1988. *The Statue of Liberty Encyclopedia* (2000), *The Encyclopedia of Ellis Island* (2004), *Ellis Island's Famous Immigrants* (2008), and *The Ellis Island Quiz Book* (2011). He also co-edited a scholarly study on world migration called *Leaving Home: Migration Yesterday and Today* (2011). His biography has been included in *Who's Who Among Hispanic Americans*, *The Directory of National Park Service Historians*, *Who's Who in America*, and *The Directory of American Scholars*. Mr. Moreno lives in New York City.

HAL MARCOVITZ has written more than 100 books for young readers. He lives in Chalfont, Pennsylvania, with his wife, Gail. They have two grown daughters, Ashley and Michelle.